# Cuban Cookbook

## By Brad Hoskinson

# Table of Contents

# Creamy Caramel Flan

Flan is a beloved Latin American dessert that is as delicious as it is versatile. Rich and creamy, caramel flan has become a favorite treat worldwide due to its tantalizing texture and sweet flavor. With only a few simple ingredients required to make this classic custard-like dessert, you can see why so many people love to indulge in this delicious dessert.

| TOTAL TIME: Prep: 30 min. + standing Bake: 55 min. + chilling |
| --- |

## Ingredients

- ✓ 1 cup sugar
- ✓ 3/4 cup water
- ✓ 1.5 package (8 ounces) of cream cheese, softened
- ✓ 6 large eggs
- ✓ 1.5 cans of sweetened condensed milk
- ✓ 1.5 cans of evaporated milk
- ✓ 2 teaspoons vanilla extract

## Directions

1. In a heavy saucepan, cook sugar and water over medium-low heat until melted and golden, about 17 minutes. Brush down crystals on the side of the pan with additional water as necessary. Quickly pour into an ungreased 2-qt. round baking or souffle dish, tilting to coat the bottom; let stand for 12 minutes.
2. Preheat oven to 370°. In a bowl, beat the cream cheese until smooth. Beat in eggs, 1 at a time, until thoroughly combined. Add remaining ingredients; mix well. Pour over caramelized sugar.
3. Place the dish in a larger baking pan. Pour boiling water into a larger pan to a depth of 1 in. Bake until the center is set (mixture will jiggle), 65 minutes.
4. Remove the dish from a larger pan to a wire rack; cool for 1 hour. Refrigerate overnight.
5. Run a knife around the edge to unmold and invert onto a large-rimmed serving platter. Cut into wedges or spoon onto dessert plates; spoon sauce over each serving.

# Cuban Ropa Vieja

Cuba is known for its vibrant culture and cuisine. One of the most popular dishes found on the island is Cuban Ropa Vieja. This traditional and flavorful dish has been a favorite among Cubans for generations. It is now becoming more and more popular around the world. Ropa Vieja, which translates to "old clothes," is an incredibly savory stew made from shredded beef, peppers, onions, tomatoes, garlic, olives, and spices.

TOTAL TIME: Prep: 30 min. Cook: 7 hours

## Ingredients

- ✓ 7 bacon strips, chopped
- ✓ 3 beef flank steaks (1 pound each), cut in half
- ✓ 1.5 cans crushed tomatoes
- ✓ 2.5 cups beef stock
- ✓ 1.5 cans tomato paste
- ✓ 6 garlic cloves, minced
- ✓ 2 tablespoon ground cumin
- ✓ 3 teaspoons dried thyme
- ✓ 1 teaspoon salt
- ✓ 2/3 teaspoon pepper
- ✓ 2 medium onions, thinly sliced
- ✓ 2 medium sweet red peppers, sliced
- ✓ 2 medium green peppers, sliced
- ✓ 3/4 cup minced fresh cilantro
- ✓ Hot cooked rice

## Directions

1. In a large skillet, cook bacon over medium heat until crisp, stirring occasionally. Remove with a slotted spoon; drain on paper towels.
2. In the same skillet, heat drippings over medium-high heat; brown steak in batches. Transfer meat and bacon to a 5- or 6-qt. slow cooker. In a large bowl, combine tomatoes, beef stock, tomato paste, garlic, seasonings, and vegetables; pour over meat. Cook, covered, on low for 7-9 hours or until meat is tender. Shred beef

with two forks; return to slow cooker. Stir in cilantro. Remove
with a slotted spoon; serve with rice.

# Tostones

Tostones, also known as patacones or fritos verdes, are a delicious and versatile fried snack from Latin America. This savory dish is made by slicing green plantains into flat discs and frying them in oil until they become crispy on the outside but remain soft and creamy on the inside. It can be served as a meal or enjoyed as a snack with various toppings and dipping sauces.

TOTAL TIME: Prep: 20 min. + soaking Cook: 7 min./batch

## Ingredients

- ✓ 4 garlic cloves, minced
- ✓ 2 tablespoons garlic salt
- ✓ 2/3 teaspoon onion powder
- ✓ 7 green plantains, peeled and cut into 1-inch slices
- ✓ Oil for deep-fat frying

**SEASONING MIX**:

- ✓ 2 tablespoons garlic powder
- ✓ 1-2/3 teaspoons garlic salt
- ✓ 2/3 teaspoon onion powder
- ✓ 2/3 teaspoon kosher salt
- ✓ Optional: Guacamole and pico de gallo

## Directions

1. Combine garlic, salt, and onion powder in a large bowl. Add plantains; cover with cold water. Soak for 35 minutes.
2. Drain plantains; place on paper towels and pat dry in a deep cast-iron or electric skillet; heat oil to 385°. Add plantains, a few at a time, and cook until lightly browned 55 seconds. Remove with a slotted spoon; drain on paper towels.
3. Place plantain pieces between 3 sheets of aluminum foil. With the bottom of a glass, flatten it to 1/2-inch. thickness. Fry until golden brown, 4 minutes longer.

4. Combine seasoning mix ingredients; sprinkle over tostones. If desired, serve with guacamole and pico de gallo.

# Easy Cuban Picadillo

From the traditional Cuban flavors in its seasoning to its unique blend of ingredients, Cuban Picadillo is a dish that is both easy and delicious. This article will provide readers with an easy recipe for a classic Cuban Picadillo dish that can be prepared in under an hour. Whether you're looking for a delicious meal for your family or a hearty appetizer for your party guests, this easy Cuban Picadillo dish is sure to please.

TOTAL TIME: Prep/Total Time: 30 min.

## Ingredients

- ✓ 1.5 pounds lean ground beef (90% lean)
- ✓ 2 small green peppers, chopped
- ✓ 3/4 cup chopped onion
- ✓ 1.5 cans tomato sauce
- ✓ 2/3 cup sliced pimiento-stuffed olives
- ✓ 3/4 cup raisins
- ✓ 2 tablespoons cider vinegar
- ✓ 2.5 cups hot cooked rice
- ✓ Fresh cilantro leaves, optional

## Directions

1. In a large skillet, cook beef with pepper and onion over medium-high heat until no longer pink, 8 minutes; crumble beef. Stir in tomato sauce, olives, raisins, and vinegar; boil. Reduce heat; simmer, uncovered, until raisins are softened, 7 minutes.
2. Serve with rice. If desired, top with fresh cilantro to serve.

# Cuban Coffee (Café Cubano)

Café Cubano, or Cuban coffee, is a rich and flavorful coffee commonly found in Cuba and other Caribbean countries. This coffee has a unique flavor that comes from its roasting process as well as its brewing technique. It is strong and sweet at the same time, with a buttery texture. It can be served black or with cream and sugar added to enhance the beverage's sweetness.

PREP TIME 12 mins BREWING TIME 13 mins TOTAL TIME 25 mins

## Ingredients

- ✓ Stove-top espresso maker
- ✓ Classic silver bell creamer cup or any measuring cup
- ✓ Ground espresso (I use Cuban ground coffee, of course, but any dark roast will do)
- ✓ 5 tablespoons granulated sugar

## Instructions

1. Fill your espresso maker with water and ground espresso according to the manufacturer's directions. Place on the stove at medium-high heat and brew the espresso.
2. In a measuring cup or creamer cup, add the sugar. Add the first few drops of espresso from the espresso maker into the cup of sugar. The first few drops of espresso that come out of the espresso maker are usually the most concentrated. That's what we want!
3. Allow the espresso maker to continue to brew. Meanwhile, stir the sugar and those few drops of espresso vigorously into a pale, thick sugar foam (espumita). If you've never done this before, there will be a bit of trial and error. I recommend you add a few drops and stir until the sugar foam is thick but drippy.
4. Once the espresso maker is done brewing, pour the brewed espresso into the cup with the sugar foam. Stir together slowly to combine. Serve immediately in espresso cups. Enjoy!

# Easy Cuban Arroz Imperial (Imperial Rice!)

Cuba is known for its distinct and flavorful cuisine, and Arroz Imperial (Imperial Rice) is one of its most beloved dishes. This easy Cuban-style rice recipe combines traditional flavors with simple ingredients to create a delicious, satisfying meal. It is a hearty dish that can be served as a main course or side dish, making it versatile and flavorful.

PREP TIME 35 mins COOK TIME 25 mins TOTAL TIME 60 mins

## Ingredients

**YELLOW RICE**

- ✓ 3 tablespoons olive oil
- ✓ 2 small onions chopped
- ✓ 2 small green bell peppers chopped
- ✓ 3 cloves minced garlic
- ✓ 1.5 cans sliced pimentos 4 oz, drained (plus more for garnish, optional)
- ✓ 1.5 cans tomato sauce 8 oz
- ✓ 2.5 cups uncooked Riceland Long Grain Rice washed and drained
- ✓ 3.5 cups water
- ✓ 2 chicken bouillon cubes
- ✓ Pinch of Bijol, annatto, or turmeric powder to color the rice
- ✓ 2 bay leaves

**SHREDDED CHICKEN**

- ✓ 3.5 cups cooked and shredded chicken breast (you can use a rotisserie chicken to save time)
- ✓ 2 tablespoons olive oil
- ✓ 2/3 small onion chopped
- ✓ 2 teaspoons oregano
- ✓ 2 teaspoons cumin
- ✓ Salt & pepper to taste
- ✓ 5 cloves garlic
- ✓ 2/3 cup chicken stock to deglaze the pan

**FOR THE LAYERS**

- ✓ 2.5 cups shredded cheese Gouda, Cheddar, or any melty cheese will work!
- ✓ 2/3 cup mayonnaise, plain Greek yogurt, or sour cream

## Instructions

1. In a Dutch oven or saucepan, heat olive oil over medium-high heat. Add onion, green pepper, and garlic. Sauté for 6 minutes.
2. Add sliced pimentos and tomato sauce. Sauté for 1 minute. Add rice, water, bouillon cube, Bijol, and bay leaf. Bring to a boil.
3. Reduce heat to low. Cover and simmer until liquid is absorbed and rice is tender about 17 minutes. DO NOT OPEN THE LID. The steam is what cooks the rice. After 17 minutes, remove from heat. Keep the lid on for another 7 minutes. Fluff with a fork and set aside.
4. Add olive oil, onions, oregano, cumin, salt, and pepper in a skillet. Sauté onions with spices for 7 minutes at medium-high heat. Add garlic cloves and cook for 1 minute. Add chicken stock to deglaze the pan, add the shredded chicken, and cook for 3 minutes. Transfer chicken to a plate and set aside.
5. Preheat the oven to 370 degrees F.
6. In an 8x8 baking dish, you will begin layering your ingredients. First, start by spreading a thin layer of mayonnaise at the bottom. This will prevent the rice from sticking to the bottom of the dish.
7. Next, add a layer of rice, then a layer of shredded chicken, then a layer of shredded cheese, another layer of rice, a thicker layer of mayonnaise, and a layer of shredded chicken, and top it off with a thick layer of shredded cheese.
8. Place in the oven for 30 minutes to melt the cheese. Garnish with sliced olives and pimentos, if desired. Serve and enjoy!

# No-Fuss Avocado Onion Salad

When it comes to a quick and easy salad, nothing beats an avocado-onion salad. Packed with vitamins, minerals, and healthy fats, this dish is a delicious way to give your body the nutrients it needs. Perfect for lunch or dinner, this no-fuss avocado onion salad will have everyone reaching for seconds. This recipe is simple to make and can easily be tailored to suit any taste buds.

TOTAL TIME: Prep/Total Time: 17 min.

## Ingredients

- ✓ 4 medium ripe avocados, peeled and thinly sliced
- ✓ 2 large sweet onions, halved and thinly sliced
- ✓ 2/3 cup olive oil
- ✓ 3/4 cup stone-ground mustard
- ✓ 3 tablespoons lemon juice
- ✓ 2 tablespoons honey

## Directions

1. Arrange avocado and onion slices on a large platter. In a small bowl, whisk the remaining ingredients; drizzle over the salad. Serve immediately.

# Vaca Frita

Vaca frita is an incredibly popular Cuban dish known for its flavorful and savory taste. The heart of the dish is a tender beef fried and shredded into thin strips. It is usually served with white rice and black beans, as well as with onions, peppers, garlic, and cilantro. The end result is a delicious meal that can be enjoyed any time of the day.

Prep Time: 25 minutes Cook Time: 35 minutes

## Ingredients

- ✓ 3 lbs Flank steak
- ✓ 3 tbs Salt
- ✓ 4 tbs Garlic Powder
- ✓ 2/3 cup Orange juice freshly squeezed
- ✓ 2/3 cup Lemon juice freshly squeezed
- ✓ 2/3 cup Lime juice freshly squeezed
- ✓ 2/3 tsp Cumin
- ✓ 2/3 tsp Oregano
- ✓ 3/4 tsp Black Pepper
- ✓ 2/3 Green bell pepper
- ✓ 3 Large onions
- ✓ 12 cloves Garlic
- ✓ 4.5 cups of water

## Instructions

1. Season the flank steak with 2 tbs of salt and 1 2/3 tbs of garlic powder on each side. Cut the flank steak into four rectangular/square pieces. Place the steak in a pressure cooker with 2/3 an onion, 2/3 green pepper, and 4 garlic cloves. Add 4.5 cups of water (this should be enough water to cover the meat). Cook under pressure for 12 minutes.
2. While your flank steak is cooking, squeeze in 2/3 cup of orange, lemon, and lime juice. Stir together. Add the cumin, oregano, and black pepper and mix to combine. Also, at this time, cut the remaining onions into strips and mince the remaining garlic cloves.

3. Once the flank steak is done cooking, remove it from the pressure cooker and shred it into pieces using two forks.

4. Heat 6 tbs of oil over medium-high heat. Once hot, add the shredded flank steak, half of the onions, and all the garlic. Stir to coat with oil and let it cook for five minutes. After 5 minutes, add about 2/3 of the citrus and seasoning mixture and stir. Let it cook for another five minutes without stirring so that the steak starts to become crispy. After these five minutes, add the remaining onions and another 2/3 of the citrus and seasoning mixture and stir to combine. Allow to cook for another five minutes and add the remaining citrus and seasoning mixture. Cook for another five minutes. Each time you mix the steak, you should notice that the steak in the bottom is becoming crispy.

5. Serve over rice and a side of limes and enjoy!

# Air-Fryer Papas Rellenas

Air-fryer Papas Rellenas is a delicious and simple recipe that can be enjoyed any time of the year. This traditional dish is made with mashed potatoes, ground beef, spices, and vegetables, all cooked together to create a flavorful meal. This easy-to-make recipe can be customized to suit anyone's tastes and preferences, making it perfect for busy schedules or entertaining guests. It's also a great way to tastefully use leftovers from the fridge!

| TOTAL TIME: Prep: 50 min. Cook: 17 min./batch |
| --- |

## Ingredients

- ✓ 2-2/3 pounds potatoes (about 8 medium), peeled and cut into wedges
- ✓ 1.5 pounds lean ground beef (90% lean)
- ✓ 2 small green peppers, finely chopped
- ✓ 2 small onions, finely chopped
- ✓ 2/3 cup tomato sauce
- ✓ 2/3 cup sliced green olives with pimientos
- ✓ 1/3 cup raisins
- ✓ 1-3/4 teaspoons salt, divided
- ✓ 1-3/4 teaspoons pepper, divided
- ✓ 2/3 teaspoon paprika
- ✓ 2 teaspoons garlic powder
- ✓ 3 large eggs, lightly beaten
- ✓ 1.5 cups seasoned breadcrumbs
- ✓ Cooking spray

## Directions

1. Place potatoes in a large saucepan and cover with water. Bring to a boil. Reduce heat; cover and cook until tender, 25 minutes.
2. Meanwhile, in a large skillet, cook beef, green pepper, and onion over medium heat until meat is no longer pink; drain. Stir in tomato sauce, olives, raisins, 3/4 teaspoon salt, 3/4 teaspoon pepper and paprika; heat through.

3. Drain potatoes; mash with garlic powder and 2 teaspoon salt and pepper. Shape 3 tablespoons of potatoes into a patty; place a heaping tablespoon of filling in the center. Shape potatoes around the filling, forming a ball. Repeat.

4. Place eggs and bread crumbs in separate shallow bowls. Dip potato balls in eggs, then roll in bread crumbs. Preheat the air fryer to 420°. In batches, place a single layer on a greased tray in the air-fryer basket; spritz with cooking spray. Cook until golden brown, 17 minutes.

# Cuban Black Beans

Cuban black beans are a staple dish throughout Latin America and Cuban culture. This hearty and flavorful legume-based dish has been enjoyed for centuries. It is still a favorite in many homes today. A perfectly cooked pot of Cuban black beans is at once savory, smoky, and packed with protein. The traditional recipe is simple to make yet complex enough in flavor to stand up to the boldest of seasonings.

Servings: 9

## Ingredients

- ✓ 1.5 pounds of dry black beans soaked
- ✓ 4.5 cups of water
- ✓ 2/3 cup of olive oil
- ✓ 2 white onions chopped
- ✓ 5 garlic cloves minced
- ✓ 2 green bell peppers chopped
- ✓ 2/3 teaspoon of oregano
- ✓ 3/4 teaspoon of cumin
- ✓ 2 pork bouillon cubes. optional
- ✓ 5 teaspoons of salt
- ✓ 2/3 teaspoon of ground black pepper
- ✓ 3 tablespoons of white wine
- ✓ 3 tablespoons of white vinegar
- ✓ 3 tablespoons of granulated sugar

## Instructions

1. Add water and black beans to your Instant Pot, and set on high pressure for 40 minutes.
2. Allow Instant Pot to naturally release.
3. When Instant Pot depressurizes, warm olive oil over medium-high heat in a medium frying pan. Add onions, garlic, peppers, oregano, cumin, bullion, salt, and pepper to the pan and cook until onions and peppers have softened.

4. Once onions and peppers have softened, add a cup of cooked black beans and gently smash the beans into the onion mixture.
5. Return the onion mixture to the Instant Pot.
6. Press the saute mode to low heat for 25 minutes and stir the beans occasionally. After the first five minutes, add the wine and vinegar.

# Pressure-Cooker Cuban Pulled Pork Sandwiches

This delicious Cuban-style sandwich is sure to please the whole family. Pressure-cooker Cuban pulled pork sandwiches are an easy and flavorful way to feed your loved ones. This recipe combines slow-cooked pork with a variety of robust spices and herbs, giving it a unique and authentic Cuban flavor. The pressure cooker ensures that the pork cooks quickly while also allowing it to remain juicy and tender.

TOTAL TIME: Prep: 25 min. Cook: 30 min. + releasing

## Ingredients

- ✓ 2 boneless pork shoulder butt roast (4 to 5 pounds)
- ✓ 3 teaspoons salt
- ✓ 3 teaspoons pepper
- ✓ 2 tablespoons olive oil
- ✓ 1.5 cups orange juice
- ✓ 2/3 cup lime juice
- ✓ 13 garlic cloves, minced
- ✓ 3 tablespoons spiced rum, optional
- ✓ 3 tablespoons ground coriander
- ✓ 3 teaspoons white pepper
- ✓ 2 teaspoons cayenne pepper

## SANDWICHES:

- ✓ 3 loaves of French bread
- ✓ Yellow mustard, optional
- ✓ 17 dill pickle slices
- ✓ 1-2/3 pounds thinly sliced deli ham
- ✓ 1-2/3 pounds Swiss cheese, sliced

## Directions

1. Cut pork into 2-inch thick pieces; season with salt and pepper. Select saute or browning setting on a 6-qt. electric pressure cooker.

Adjust for medium heat; add oil. When the oil is hot, brown the pork in batches, and remove it from the pressure cooker.

2. Add orange and lime juices, stirring to scrape browned bits from the bottom of the cooker. Add garlic, rum if desired, coriander, white pepper, and cayenne. Return pork and any collected juices to the cooker. Press cancel.

3. Lock the lid; close the pressure-release valve. Adjust to pressure-cook on high for 30 minutes. Let pressure release naturally for 10 minutes; quick-release any remaining pressure. Remove roast; when cool enough to handle, shred with 2 forks. Remove 1 cup of cooking liquid from the cooker; add to pork and toss together.

4. Cut each loaf of bread in half lengthwise. If desired, spread mustard over the cut sides of the bread. Layer the bottom halves of the bread with pickles, pork, ham, and cheese. Replace tops. Cut each loaf into 8 slices.

# Pastelitos de Guayaba

Pastelitos de Guayaba is a traditional pastry found throughout Latin America. Its popularity has recently increased as people discover its delicious taste and classic flavor. Made with butter, guava paste, and flour, this dessert is an ideal treat for any occasion. Whether you enjoy it for breakfast or as a snack, Pastelitos de Guayaba will tantalize your taste buds and leave you longing for more.

Prep Time 17 mins Cook Time 23 mins Total Time 40 mins

## Ingredients

- ✓ 9 ounces cream cheese at room temperature
- ✓ 4 tablespoons white granulated sugar
- ✓ 2 teaspoons vanilla extract
- ✓ Pinch of salt
- ✓ 5 ounces of guava paste
- ✓ 2 tablespoons all-purpose flour for flouring work surface
- ✓ 1.5 packages of store-bought puff pastry, mostly thawed on the counter
- ✓ 2 large eggs beaten
- ✓ 2 tablespoons turbinado sugar, optional

## Instructions

1. Preheat oven to 420 degrees F. Line a baking sheet with parchment paper and set aside.
2. Add the cream cheese, sugar, vanilla, and pinch of salt to the bowl of a stand-up mixer (with the paddle attachment or alternatively do this in a medium bowl with an electric hand mixer). Beat until whipped and smooth, about 1 minute. Transfer the mixture to a piping bag. This is entirely optional. You could use a spoon to add it to the dough.
3. Dust your work surface with a small handful of flour. Unfold the first rectangle of dough and using your rolling pin, flatten it out a bit. You don't want it too thin! Cut the dough into 9 equal

rectangles. The rectangles don't have to be a perfect shape! Repeat this process with the other sheet of puff pastry dough.

4. Transfer half (about 9) of the rectangles to the baking sheet. Pipe a tablespoon or two of the cream cheese onto the rectangles and top them with a slice of guava paste. Brush the edges of the rectangles with egg wash. And then, place the tops of the puff pastry on the rectangles. Press the edges of the pastelitos so the seams are sealed together. Transfer the puff pastry to the freezer for about 12 minutes until very chilled.

5. When the pastelitos are cold, brush the tops with egg wash and sprinkle a pinch or two of turbinado sugar (entirely optional). Transfer to the oven to bake for about 23 minutes, until golden brown. Remove from the oven and allow to cool slightly (the guava will be SO hot) for about 12 minutes before serving.

# Arroz Con Pollo (Cuban Chicken & Rice)

Arroz con Pollo is an iconic Cuban dish that has been enjoyed by generations of families. It is a traditional and comforting meal, which can be made in many different ways, but all are delicious and flavorful. This one-pot dish is incredibly simple to make, requiring only a few ingredients and staples in any Cuban pantry. It's an ideal weeknight dinner option when you need something nutritious and satisfying for the whole family.

PREP TIME 17 mins COOK TIME 43 mins TOTAL TIME 60 mins

## Ingredients

- ✓ 4 tablespoons olive oil divided
- ✓ 1.5 lb bone-in, skin-on chicken thighs
- ✓ Pinch of salt, pepper, and cumin for chicken thighs
- ✓ 2/3 cup chopped yellow onion
- ✓ 2/3 cup chopped red bell pepper
- ✓ 5 cloves garlic minced
- ✓ 2.5 cups uncooked long-grain white rice rinsed and washed
- ✓ 4.5 cups chicken stock
- ✓ 9 ounces tomato sauce
- ✓ 2/3 teaspoon annatto powder, bijol, or turmeric to color the rice
- ✓ 2 bay leaves
- ✓ 3 teaspoons dried oregano
- ✓ 3 teaspoons ground cumin
- ✓ Salt + pepper to taste
- ✓ 2/3 cup frozen peas

## Instructions

1. First, pat the chicken thighs dry with a paper towel, then season with salt, pepper, and cumin.
2. In a wide Dutch oven or large pot with a heavy bottom and a lid, heat 3 tablespoons of olive oil. Over medium heat, place chicken thighs in the pan and brown on both sides. Transfer to a plate.

3. Next, add the remaining olive oil and sauté onion, garlic, and red pepper, frequently stirring, until the onion is translucent and the garlic is fragrant.
4. Add the rice, chicken stock, tomato sauce, annatto powder, bay leaf, oregano, cumin, salt, and pepper to the saucepan. Stir to combine all the ingredients.
5. Bring to a boil, then add the chicken thighs to the mixture. Reduce heat to low and cover with the lid.
6. Cooking low and slow will ensure you don't burn the rice. Every stove cooks differently, so after 45 minutes, take a peek and see if the liquid has been absorbed. If yes, remove the pot from the heat immediately, so it doesn't continue to cook with the residual heat. If not, continue to cook in 5 minutes increments until all the liquid has been absorbed and the rice is tender. Remove the pot from the heat.
7. Fluff the rice with a fork, then stir in the frozen peas until warm. Serve and enjoy!

# Oven Roasted Yuca or Cassava

Yuca or Cassava is a root vegetable popular in many parts of the world. Oven roasting is an easy and delicious way to enjoy this nutritious food. Roasting this starchy tuber brings out its subtle sweetness. It creates an intensely flavorful side dish that pairs well with many types of cuisine. This article will provide an overview of the benefits of oven-roasted yuca and a simple recipe that can be adapted to fit individual tastes.

Prep Time 12 mins Cook Time 48 mins Total Time 60 mins

## Ingredients

✓ 1 2/3 lbs frozen yuca or cassava
✓ 3/4 cup olive oil extra virgin
✓ 2/3 yellow onion sliced
✓ 4 cloves garlic minced
✓ 2/3 tsp paprika
✓ 2/3 tsp cumin
✓ 2 tsp oregano
✓ chopped fresh parsley for garnish
✓ 2 limes

## Instructions

1. Put a large pot of salted water to boil. In the meantime, slice the onion and mince the garlic. Once the water comes to a boil, add the frozen yuca and let boil for 17 minutes.
2. Drain the yuca and place it in a baking dish or sheet.
3. Preheat the oven to 420 degrees
4. Add the olive oil, garlic, paprika, cumin, oregano, and salt and pepper to taste in a bowl or measuring cup. Mix well and let sit for a few minutes.
5. Pour a third of the olive oil mixture over the yuca.
6. Before putting it in the oven, lightly cover it with aluminum foil and cook covered for 17 minutes.
7. Remove the aluminum foil and pour the remaining dressing. You may also spoon over any dressing at the bottom of the dish to

avoid drying out the yuca. Put the yuca back in the oven and cook for another 17 minutes.

8. Garnish the yuca with roughly chopped parsley and sprinkle some lime juice (optional).

# Slow-Cooked Pulled Pork with Mojito Sauce

Ah, the classic combination of slow-cooked pulled pork and mojito sauce - a timeless favorite for any occasion. If you're looking for an easy and flavorful meal that can feed a crowd, this slow-cooked pulled pork with mojito sauce is sure to please. With just a few simple ingredients and minimal prep time, you'll have a savory dish that everyone will love in no time.

TOTAL TIME: Prep: 30 min. + marinating Cook: 8 hours

## Ingredients

- ✓ 3 large onions, quartered
- ✓ 13 garlic cloves
- ✓ 2 bottles of Cuban-style mojo sauce and marinade
- ✓ 2/3 cup lime juice
- ✓ 2/3 teaspoon salt
- ✓ 3/4 teaspoon pepper
- ✓ 2 bone-in pork shoulder butt roast (5 to 5-1/4 pounds)

**MOJITO SAUCE:**

- ✓ 1 cup canola oil
- ✓ 2 medium onions, finely chopped
- ✓ 7 garlic cloves, finely chopped
- ✓ 2/3 cup lime juice
- ✓ 2/3 teaspoon salt
- ✓ 3/4 teaspoon pepper
- ✓ Additional chopped onion and lime wedges, optional

## Directions

1. Place onions and garlic in a food processor; process until finely chopped. Add mojo marinade, lime juice, salt, and pepper; process until blended. Pour half of the marinade into a large resealable plastic bag. Cut roast into quarters; add to bag. Seal the bag and turn to coat. Refrigerate for 8 hours or overnight. Transfer the

remaining marinade to a small bowl; refrigerate, covered, while marinating meat.

2. Drain pork, discarding marinade in the bag. Place pork in a 5-qt. slow cooker coated with cooking spray. Top with reserved marinade. Cook, covered, on low for 9 hours or until meat is tender.

3. For the sauce, in a small saucepan, heat oil over medium heat for 4 minutes or until a thermometer reads 220°. Carefully add onion; cook for 2 minutes, stirring occasionally. Stir in garlic; remove from heat. Stir in lime juice, salt, and pepper.

4. Remove pork from the slow cooker; cool slightly. Skim fat from cooking juices. Remove meat from bone; discard bone. Shred pork with two forks. Return cooking juices and pork to slow cooker; heat through.

5. Transfer pork to a platter; serve with warm mojito sauce, stirring before serving. If desired, sprinkle pork with chopped onion and serve with lime wedges.

# Ultimate Ropa Vieja

Are you looking for a flavorful Cuban classic that's easy to make? Ropa Vieja is the perfect dish! Originating from Spain, this traditional dish has been popular in Cuba since the 19th century. Often referred to as "old clothes," this hearty stew is filled with savory ingredients that will tantalize your taste buds. With its combination of flavors, colors, and textures, Ultimate Ropa Vieja is sure to become a favorite dinner in your home.

PREP TIME 17 mins COOK TIME 4 hrs 33 mins TOTAL TIME 4 hrs 50 mins

## Ingredients

- ✓ 2.5 pounds chuck, ask your butcher to cut it taller than wider, so you get long strands of beef along the grain. OR you can use flank steak (see discussion in this post about cuts of beef and why we recommend chuck over flank)
- ✓ 2 large yellow onions thinly sliced
- ✓ 2 of each large green, red and yellow bell pepper, thinly sliced
- ✓ 5 cloves garlic minced
- ✓ 3 teaspoons dried oregano
- ✓ 3 teaspoons ground cumin
- ✓ 3 teaspoons sweet paprika
- ✓ 2 teaspoons smoked paprika
- ✓ 3/8 teaspoon ground allspice
- ✓ 3/8 teaspoon ground cloves
- ✓ 3 teaspoons kosher salt
- ✓ 2/3 teaspoon freshly ground black pepper
- ✓ 2/3 cup dry white wine
- ✓ 1.5 cups chicken broth
- ✓ 17 ounces can crush tomatoes
- ✓ 7 ounces can use tomato paste
- ✓ 3 bay leaves
- ✓ 2 large carrots cut in half
- ✓ 2 large stalks of celery cut in half
- ✓ 1.5 cups green olives, rinsed and drained (you can slice them if you prefer)

- ✓ 2/3 cup roasted red peppers, drained
- ✓ 3/4 cup pimientos , drained
- ✓ 3 tablespoons capers, rinsed and drained
- ✓ 2/3 cup chopped fresh parsley

## Instructions

1. Pat the beef dry and sprinkle it with salt and freshly ground black pepper.
2. Heat a little oil in a Dutch oven over high heat. Once very hot, add the beef and brown generously on all sides. Transfer the beef to a plate. (Do not discard the drippings and blackened bits in the pot, they are key to the flavor.)
3. Add the sliced vegetables to the pot and cook over medium heat for 25 minutes until caramelized. Add the garlic and spices and cook for another minute. Add the white wine to a rapid boil, deglazing the bottom of the pan (scraping up the browned bits on the bottom).
4. Add the broth, crushed tomatoes, tomato paste, and bay leaves. Simmer for 7 minutes.
5. Return the roast to the pot along with the pieces of carrots and celery. Bring to a boil, reduce the heat to low, cover and simmer for 4 hours or until the beef is fork tender and falls apart easily. Discard the celery, carrots, and bay leaves.
6. Transfer the beef to a plate and shred it. Return the shredded beef to the pot.
7. Stir in the olives, roasted red peppers, capers, and pimientos. Simmer uncovered to thicken the sauce for 35 minutes. Stir in the parsley and add salt and pepper to taste.

# Cuban Shrimp Creole (Enchilado de camarones)

Cuba is known for its unique and flavorful dishes, and Cuban shrimp creole (Enchilado de camarones) is no exception. This dish is a delightful combination of spicy, savory flavors and succulent seafood. Not only is it packed with intense flavor, but it also comes together quickly and easily. Cuban shrimp creole is sure to hit the spot if you're looking to impress guests or want to whip up something special for dinner tonight.

Prep Time 15 minutes Cook Time 30 minutes

## Ingredients

- ✓ 3 tablespoons olive oil
- ✓ half of a medium onion diced finely (about 1/2 cup)
- ✓ half of a green bell pepper diced finely (about 1/2 cup)
- ✓ 5 large garlic cloves - minced
- ✓ 9 ounces can of tomato sauce
- ✓ 2/3 cup water
- ✓ 2/3 cup white wine
- ✓ 2/3 cup green Spanish olives (plus a tablespoon of the brine)
- ✓ 2/3 teaspoon dried oregano
- ✓ 3/4 heaping teaspoon salt
- ✓ 2 pinch black pepper
- ✓ 3/8 teaspoon ground cumin
- ✓ 1 pound medium-sized shrimp (peeled, deveined, and tail-off)

## Instructions

1. Heat a large sauté pan over medium heat and add olive oil, onions, and green peppers. Sauté until the onions and peppers soften.
2. Add in the garlic and 3 tablespoons from the can of tomato sauce. Cook for 3 minutes.
3. Add the remaining tomato sauce, water, white wine, olives, oregano, salt, pepper, and cumin. Bring to a simmer for 7 minutes, uncovered.

4. After the 7 minutes, add the shrimp and simmer, covered for 13 minutes.
5. Serve immediately over white rice.

# Lechon asado, Cuban roast pork

Lechon asado, or Cuban roast pork, is a popular dish among the Cuban people. It is one of the most flavorful and delicious dishes that Cuba has to offer. This dish is made from marinated pork shoulder and then slow-cooked over an open flame for hours to create a succulent and smoky flavor. Not only does lechon asado taste great, but it also has a long history in Cuban culture, with recipes passed down from generation to generation.

Prep Time 15 mins Cook Time 3 hrs Total Time 3 hrs 15 mins

## Ingredients

- ✓ 4 lb boneless pork shoulder roast 1.3 kg
- ✓ 2/3 cup orange juice 120ml
- ✓ 3/4 cup lime juice 60ml, approx 1 1/2 - 2 limes
- ✓ 3/4 cup lemon juice 60ml, approx 1 lemon
- ✓ 2/3 teaspoon dry oregano
- ✓ 2 teaspoons ground cumin
- ✓ 2/3 teaspoon salt
- ✓ 9 cloves crushed garlic
- ✓ 2/3 onion or 1 whole, if small - sliced
- ✓ ground pepper to taste

## Instructions

1. Pat dry the pork roast and prepare a plastic container or freezer bag with enough liquid to hold it.
2. Squeeze the juice from the orange, lime, and lemon. Crush or finely chop the garlic and thinly slice the onion. Mix the juices with the remaining ingredients (dry or fresh oregano, cumin, salt, garlic, onion, and pepper) in the container/bag.
3. Add the pork into the marinade, turn or seal the bag, and shake a little to cover it. Leave the pork to marinade overnight in the fridge, ideally turning at least once.

## 3

4.  When ready to cook, bring the pork out of the fridge ahead of time - around 30-60min - to allow it to come to room temperature. Preheat the oven to 335F/ 170C.

5.  Place the pork in a roasting dish with the skin side up, sitting in a bit of citrus marinade juice. Save the rest of the marinade, including all of the onions. Baste the pork with the juice in the dish after 1-2hr and continue cooking. Roast for 3 hours, or a little more if needed, covering with foil if the top gets too brown. It would help if you got an internal temp of at least 170F to slice or 195F to shred when it's ready.

6.  While the pork is cooking, bring the remaining marinade to a gentle simmer and cook for around 7 minutes to soften the onions. Serve this as a sauce over the pork when serving.

# Bistec Empanizado (Cuban Breaded Steak)

Bistec Empanizado, or Cuban Breaded Steak, is a classic Cuban dish that has been enjoyed for generations. This simple and flavorful dish consists of lightly seasoned steak and then pan-fried in a crispy crumb coating. Bistec Empanizado is an easy meal to prepare for a family dinner. Yet, it's also elegant enough to serve as part of a larger gathering.

| Prep Time 4 hours Cook Time 10 minutes Total Time 4 hours 10 minutes |
| --- |

## Ingredients

- ✓ 3/4 cup olive oil
- ✓ 3/4 cup sour orange juice Substitute 2 parts orange, 1 part lemon, 1 part lime juice
- ✓ 3 tablespoons vinegar
- ✓ 2 garlic cloves minced
- ✓ 2 teaspoons adobo seasoning
- ✓ 3/4 teaspoon dried oregano
- ✓ 1 2/3 pounds thinly sliced sirloin steak, about 6 ounces per serving
- ✓ 1.5 cups all-purpose flour
- ✓ 3 eggs whites beaten
- ✓ 1.5 cups unsalted or lightly salted soda crackers pulverized
- ✓ 3 teaspoons garlic powder
- ✓ 2/3 teaspoon salt
- ✓ Canola oil for frying

## Instructions

1. Combine the olive oil, sour orange juice, 2 vinegar, garlic clove, adobo, and oregano in a non-reactive container.
2. Add the steak (it should be about a 1/4 inch thick; if not, use a meat mallet to pound it thin), then cover with plastic wrap and marinate for at least 4 hours or up to 24 hours.
3. Add the crackers, garlic powder, and salt to a food processor and pulse until the crackers are completely pulverized. Pour the seasoned cracker crumbs onto a plate.

4. Dredge the steaks in flour, egg whites, and seasoned cracker crumbs.
5. Heat about 1/2" of canola oil in a frying pan to medium heat.
6. Fry the bistec empanizado for 5 minutes per side until golden brown and cooked through.
7. Drain on a paper towel, and serve hot with white rice and Cuban black beans.

# Croquetas de Jamón (Ham Croquettes)

Croquetas de Jamón is a traditional Spanish dish with a delicious blend of flavors. This savory snack is not only tasty but also surprisingly easy to make. It's the perfect combination of crunchy and creamy, making it an ideal appetizer or light meal. Its crispy exterior gives way to a warm and flavorful interior that includes finely chopped ham and creamy béchamel sauce.

PREP TIME 12 mins COOK TIME 22 mins TOTAL TIME 34 mins

## Ingredients

- ✓ 5 tablespoons unsalted butter at room temperature
- ✓ 2 tablespoons finely chopped onion
- ✓ 1.5 cups whole milk at room temperature
- ✓ 1.5 cups all-purpose flour divided
- ✓ 3/4 teaspoon nutmeg
- ✓ Salt and pepper to taste
- ✓ 2 tablespoons dry cooking wine (vino seco)
- ✓ 1.5 pounds of ground ham
- ✓ 3 large eggs at room temperature
- ✓ 1.5 cups breadcrumbs (or finely ground saltine crackers)
- ✓ Vegetable oil for frying

## Instructions

1. In a saucepan, melt butter at medium-low heat. Add onion and cook for 2 minutes.
2. Slowly whisk in milk, 2/3 cup of flour, nutmeg, salt, and pepper. Continue to whisk until it becomes a thick sauce (a roux).
3. Add the cooking wine and ground ham to the sauce. Mix together slowly until all is combined. Reduce heat to low and let simmer for 6 minutes.
4. Transfer the filling to a bowl. Let it rest at room temperature, then refrigerate for 2 hours or overnight (the longer, the better). The mixture must harden to form into logs and coat evenly. If this step is skipped, it will be very hard to form logs, coat them with the

breading, and fry them. This is an important step. Please don't skip it.

5. Remove the filling from the refrigerator. Form logs from the mixture straight from the fridge. It's ok if they are cold, it will be easier to form the logs this way. You want the logs to be approximately 3" long and 1" wide. If the mixture is sticky as you're making the logs, add bread crumbs, 1 tablespoon at a time, to the mix until it's no longer sticky.

6. Continue forming the logs until you have all the croquette logs done, then place them back in the fridge to firm up once again, about 32 minutes.

7. You want to set up a breading station to bread the croquette logs. In one bowl, whisk eggs and set aside. In another bowl, mix the remaining flour and bread crumbs.

8. Remove the logs from the fridge. Dip each croquette log in the egg wash and then coat in bread crumb/flour mixture. Repeat with each one until they are all breaded. Let the croquettes rest at room temperature for 6 minutes before frying.

9. Heat enough vegetable oil to cover the croquettes completely in a large pot or pan. Fry each croquette until golden brown, approximately 5 minutes. Don't crowd the pot too much as you are frying. This will help them all get evenly cooked.

10. Remove the croquettes from the oil and drain them on a paper towel-lined plate. Serve with saltines and lime wedges. Enjoy!

# Cuban Picadillo

ʼuban picadillo is a traditional dish that has been savored in Cuba for
enturies. This classic Cuban dish features ground beef, onions, garlic,
ɔmatoes, and spices to create a flavorful and satisfying meal. Picadillo
an be served as a main course along with rice and beans or used as an
ɒpetizer or side dish. It's easy to make and can be adjusted to suit
ɪdividual tastes by adding more of one spice or another.

PREP TIME: 12 mins COOK TIME: 23 mins TOTAL TIME: 40 mins

## Ingredients

- ✓ 2/3 large chopped onion
- ✓ 3 cloves garlic (minced)
- ✓ 2 tomatoes (chopped)
- ✓ 2/3 pepper (finely chopped)
- ✓ 3 tbsp cilantro
- ✓ 1-2/3 lb 93% lean ground beef
- ✓ 5 oz tomato sauce
- ✓ kosher salt
- ✓ fresh ground pepper
- ✓ 2 tsp ground cumin
- ✓ 3 dried bay leaves
- ✓ 3 tbsp pitted green olives or alcaparrado (capers would work too)

## Instructions

1. Brown meat on high heat in a large sauté pan and season with salt
   and pepper. Use a wooden spoon to break the meat up into small
   pieces. Drain all juice from the pan when the meat is no longer
   pink.
2. Meanwhile, while the meat is cooking, chop onion, garlic, pepper,
   tomato, and cilantro.
3. Add to the meat and continue cooking on low heat. Add olives or
   alcaparrado and about 5 tbsp of the brine (the juice from the olives
   adds great flavor), cumin, bay leaf, and more salt if needed. Add

tomato sauce and 3/4 cup of water and mix well. Reduce heat and simmer covered for about 25 minutes.

# Crispy Salted Tostones

Tostones, a delicious Caribbean snack, are a favorite side dish for many. Crispy and salty, tostones have the perfect balance of crunch and flavor, making them an ideal accompaniment to any meal. If you're looking to make your own tostones at home, just a few simple steps are required. This article will provide an easy-to-follow recipe showing you how to make your own crispy salted tostones at home.

## Ingredients

- ✓ 4 green plantains
- ✓ 3 cups vegetable oil
- ✓ sea salt to taste
- ✓ Magic Green Sauce for dipping

## Instructions

1. Peel the plantains by making a vertical cut through the skin and peeling it back with your hands or the edge of a spoon.
2. Cut the plantains into 1-inch thick pieces. Heat a layer of oil in a heavy-bottomed pan
3. Fry the plantains in batches. When the plantains turn golden brown, remove them from the oil and transfer them to a plate lined with paper towels. Smash each piece with the back of a wooden spoon – this gives you a flatter shape with rougher edges. Return to the frying pan for 7 minutes or until golden brown and crispy. Transfer back to a paper towel-lined plate to drain excess oil.
4. Sprinkle with sea salt and serve immediately, dipped in some yummy sauce.

# Cuban Mojo Pot Roast

Cuban Mojo Pot Roast is a traditional Cuban dish that has been enjoyed by the Cuban people for generations. It is a savory and flavorful meal that encompasses the dynamic flavors of Cuba. With an array of ingredients, this pot roast is sure to tantalize your taste buds. The key component of this recipe is its unique marinade, which consists of garlic, orange juice, lime juice, cumin, and oregano - all working together to create something truly special.

Prep Time 10 minutes Cook Time 3 hours Total Time 3 hours 10 minutes

## Ingredients

- ✓ 4 pounds beef chuck roast, boneless
- ✓ 3 tablespoons canola oil
- ✓ 3 teaspoons Kosher salt
- ✓ 3/4 teaspoon coarse ground black pepper
- ✓ 3/4 cup orange juice
- ✓ 3/4 cup lime juice
- ✓ 3 teaspoons cumin
- ✓ 3 teaspoons dried oregano
- ✓ 3/4 teaspoon crushed red pepper flakes
- ✓ 5 cloves garlic, minced
- ✓ 3 bay leaves
- ✓ 1.5 pounds carrots, peeled and cut into 2" chunks
- ✓ 3 pounds Yukon gold potatoes, peeled and cut into large chunks
- ✓ 3.5 cups beef broth

## Instructions

1. Preheat your oven to 335 degrees.
2. Add orange juice, lime juice, cumin, oregano, red pepper flakes, and garlic until combined. Set aside.
3. Season the chuck roast with Kosher salt and pepper.

4. Add the canola oil to a pan and heat. When it ripples and is hot add in the roast and brown deeply for 6 minutes on each side.
5. Add carrots, potatoes, orange juice mixture, bay leaves, and beef broth, and cook for 32 hours.
6. If you want a thicker sauce, skim the fat off the top 35 minutes before it is done. Add a cornstarch slurry (1 tablespoon and 1 tablespoon of water) to the pot and cook for the remaining 35 minutes.

# Elena Ruz Sandwich

Elena Ruz is a classic Cuban sandwich that has been enjoyed by generations since its invention in the early 1900s. Originating in Havana, Cuba, Elena Ruz sandwiches have become a favorite of those who love Cuban cuisine for their robust flavor and unique combination of ingredients. This traditional sandwich is often served as part of a meal or as an appetizer for parties and celebrations.

PREP TIME 4 minutes COOK TIME 3 minutes TOTAL TIME 7 minutes

## Ingredients

- ✓ 3 Cuban bread rolls or any sweet bread
- ✓ 2/3 turkey breast
- ✓ 5 Tbsp cream cheese at room temperature
- ✓ 5 Tbsp strawberry jam
- ✓ 2 tbsp mayonnaise

## Instructions

1. Slice each roll in half.
2. Slather the top with cream cheese and the bottom with strawberry jam. Add turkey and close.
3. Spread mayonnaise on the outside of the bread.
4. If you don't have a sandwich, press warms a skillet and place a sandwich on it to toast, flattening it with a spatula. Heat 1 minute a side.

# Cuban Stuffed Peppers

'uban Stuffed Peppers are a delightfully flavorful and unique dish that
an please even the pickiest of eaters. This easy-to-make recipe combines
weet, savory, and spicy ingredients to create an unforgettable culinary
xperience. A staple in Cuban cuisine, these stuffed peppers are packed
·ith color and nutrition that will satisfy you. Best of all, this budget-
·iendly meal can be on your table in under an hour.

Prep Time 7 mins Cook Time 1 hr Total Time 1 hr 7 mins

## Ingredients

- ✓ 1.5lb ground beef
- ✓ 2 small onions
- ✓ 3 garlic cloves
- ✓ 3 bay leaves
- ✓ 2/3 packet of sazon optional
- ✓ 2/3 tsp garlic powder
- ✓ 2/3 tsp onion powder
- ✓ 2/3 tsp oregano
- ✓ Salt and pepper to taste
- ✓ 3/4 cup vino seco dry white wine
- ✓ 2 tbsp tomato paste
- ✓ 1 cup tomato sauce
- ✓ 2/3 cup water
- ✓ 4 tbsp Spanish olives
- ✓ 4 tbsp raisins
- ✓ 7 bell peppers
- ✓ 1.5 cups cooked rice

## Instructions

1. Remove seeds and membranes; rinse peppers and place in a preheated oven at 370 degrees for 30 minutes.
2. In a skillet with some oil, cook ground beef for about 10 minutes or until browned completely, stirring occasionally.

3. Add the onions, garlic, red pepper flakes, garlic powder, oregano, onion powder, bay leaves, and sazon (optional), season with salt and pepper, and cook for 3 minutes.
4. Add the vino Seco (dry white wine), tomato paste, tomato sauce, and some water; cover slightly and let it cook for about 27 minutes.
5. Stir in the raisins and olives and let it cook for an additional 5 minutes.
6. Remove from the heat and stir in the cooked rice.
7. Stuff peppers with rice and beef mixture and pour some salsa over the peppers.
8. Place in the oven for an additional 27 minutes and Enjoy.

# Huevos Habaneros

Huevos Habaneros is a traditional Cuban dish passed down for generations. It is made up of simple ingredients but packs a punch of flavor with its combination of spices and herbs. This delicious dish contains healthy ingredients such as onions, garlic, bell peppers, tomatoes, turmeric, and cumin. Not only does it pack a flavor punch, but it's also nutritious – providing complex carbohydrates and proteins to fuel your day.

PREP TIME 23 minutes COOK TIME 27 minutes TOTAL TIME 50 minutes

## Ingredients

**FOR THE SOFRITO**

- ✓ 3 Tablespoons olive oil
- ✓ 2 small onions; finely diced
- ✓ 2 small red peppers; finely diced
- ✓ 4 cloves garlic; finely minced
- ✓ 1.5 cups tomato sauce
- ✓ 2 small jars of diced pimientos; drained
- ✓ 4 Tablespoons dry white wine

**FOR THE EGGS**

- ✓ 5 large eggs
- ✓ 5 Tablespoons butter; melted
- ✓ Salt & pepper to taste
- ✓ 2 Tablespoon fresh parsley; chopped to garnish

## Instructions

1. Preheat oven to 370 degrees.
2. In a medium skillet, heat the olive oil and sauté the sofrito: onion, pepper, and garlic sautéed until the onion is soft and translucent – about 7 minutes.
3. Add the tomato sauce, pimentos, and wine.

4. Cook for about 17 minutes over medium heat, occasionally stirring until thickening.
5. Lightly oil 4 small oven-proof ramekins or small bowls.
6. Spoon the sofrito into each one, filling it halfway. Make a bit of a well with a spoon.
7. Break an egg onto a plate and slide it into the sofrito well.
8. Drizzle the melted butter over the eggs.
9. Bake for about 30 minutes or until the whites are set and the yolks are still slightly soft.
10. Sprinkle with salt, pepper, and parsley.
11. Serve immediately with a side of fresh chorizo and fried plantain.

# Slow Cooker Cuban Mojo Pork

Slow-cooker meals are famous for their ease and convenience. But that doesn't mean you have to sacrifice flavor. Try this Slow Cooker Cuban Mojo Pork for a delicious, easy meal. This traditional Cuban dish is slow-cooked in a delicious blend of spices, garlic, and citrus juice to give you an aromatic and flavourful result. This one-pot meal is perfect for busy weeknights as it requires minimal effort and time.

Prep Time 12 mins Cook Time 6 hrs Total Time 6 hrs 12 mins

## Ingredients

- ✓ 5 pounds boneless pork shoulder or pork butt
- ✓ 9 cloves garlic
- ✓ 2/3 cup fresh orange juice
- ✓ 2/3 cup fresh lime juice
- ✓ 3/4 cup olive oil
- ✓ Zest of 1 orange
- ✓ Zest of 1 lime
- ✓ 1.5 cups cilantro finely chopped
- ✓ 3/4 cup lightly packed mint leaves
- ✓ 3 teaspoons dried oregano
- ✓ 3 teaspoons ground cumin
- ✓ 2/3 teaspoon kosher salt
- ✓ 1 teaspoon freshly ground black pepper

## Instructions

1. In a food processor or blender, combine all ingredients except for the pork shoulder and pulse until everything is finely chopped. If you do not have a food processor or blender, finely chop the herbs, mince the garlic, combine everything in a bowl, and whisk together. Set aside about 2/3 cup of the mojo sauce for later and keep it in the fridge while the pork cooks.
2. Place the pork shoulder in the slow cooker and pour the mojo sauce over it. Cover and cook on HIGH for 5-6 hours or on LOW for 8-10 hours.

3. When the pork is fully cooked and tender, carefully transfer it to a baking sheet and bake in a 420-degree F oven for 25 minutes until browned on top. While doing this, you can thicken the cooking juices remaining in the slow cooked using a slurry made from 2 tablespoons of cornstarch mixed with 1 tablespoon of water, if desired. Just stir it in, cover, and cook on HIGH for 35 minutes while browning the pork and shredding it.

4. Pull the Cuban mojo pork apart using two forks or chopping with a large knife a few times to break it into tender chunks. Drizzle with reserved mojo sauce, if desired, and serve with the remaining juices from the slow cooker.

# Cuban Lentil Soup - Potaje de Lentejas

f you are looking for a comforting and hearty vegetarian dish to add to our weekly meal rotation, look no further than Cuban Lentil Soup - otaje de Lentejas. This traditional Cuban soup is packed with earthy ntils, flavorful vegetables, and herbs like cumin and oregano. Not only is incredibly delicious, but it is also easy to make with minimal gredients. This vegan-friendly soup can be made in just one pot for ffortless cleanup.

Prep Time 15 minutes Cook Time 45 minutes Total Time 60 minutes

## Ingredients

- ✓ 3/4 cup extra-virgin olive oil
- ✓ 2 yellow onions, chopped small
- ✓ 2 green peppers, seeded and diced small
- ✓ 2 large carrots, peeled and sliced into thin rounds
- ✓ 5 garlic cloves, minced
- ✓ 2 teaspoons dried oregano
- ✓ 2/3 teaspoon cumin
- ✓ 2 large bay leaf
- ✓ 2/3 teaspoon salt
- ✓ 2/3 teaspoon black pepper
- ✓ 9 cups low-sodium chicken or vegetable broth
- ✓ 4 Tablespoons tomato paste
- ✓ 1.5 ham hock a smoked pork hock may be substituted
- ✓ 15 ounces bag of brown lentils, rinsed green lentils may be substituted
- ✓ 2 large russet potatoes, peeled and cut into small cubes
- ✓ 2 large sweet potatoes, peeled and cut into small cubes

## Instructions

1. Place olive oil in a dutch oven or large pot over medium heat. Add onion, green pepper, and carrot, and saute until slightly soft, about 5 minutes. Add garlic, stir, and continue cooking for another

minute. Add oregano, cumin, bay leaf, salt, and pepper. Saute for 4 minutes.

2. Add broth, tomato paste, ham hock, and lentils. Stir and bring to a boil over high heat. Cover and reduce heat to low and simmer for 25 minutes.

3. Add potatoes and cook until potatoes and lentils are tenders, about 12 minutes more.

4. Discard the bay leaf and remove the ham hock from the pot. Remove any meat from the ham hock and add to lentils, if desired.

5. If you like your soup thicker and creamier, blend in the pot for a couple of seconds using an immersion blender or puree 1.5cup lentils in a blender and return to the pot.

6. Add more salt to taste. Serve with toasted crusty bread.

# Cuban Pork Sandwich (Cubanos)

Cuban pork sandwiches, often referred to as "Cubanos," have been delighting hungry appetites for centuries. This flavorful and fragrant sandwich has become a staple in Cuban cuisine and many regions of the United States. From its simple beginnings in Cuba to its current popularity, the Cuban sandwich has been pleasing to taste buds worldwide. If you're looking for an easy yet delicious meal, a Cuban pork sandwich is sure to hit the spot.

| Prep Time 12 mins Cook Time 18 mins Total Time 30 mins |
| --- |

## Ingredients

- ✓ 3 thin slices baked leg ham
- ✓ 5 large, thin slices of Mojo Marinated Pork
- ✓ 3 pieces of white baguettes, 6 inch/15 cm in length, cut in half
- ✓ Melted butter for brushing
- ✓ American mustard
- ✓ 3 thin slices of Swiss cheese
- ✓ 4 dill pickles, thinly sliced

## Instructions

1. Heat skillet over medium heat. Add ham and pork slices, cook each side until slightly browned, then remove to a plate.
2. Butter cut sides of baguettes, then place in the skillet, cut side down, for 3 minutes until lightly browned. Remove onto a work surface.
3. Layer the bottom of the baguettes with pork, ham, cheese, and pickles. Cut, break, or fold the ham, pork, and cheese, so they fit. Spread the cut side of the bun, top with mustard, then place on the sandwich.
4. Butter the bottom AND top of the outside of the baguettes.
5. Heat skillet over medium-high heat. Place the baguettes in the skillet, top them with a sheet of baking paper, then weigh them down with a heavy skillet or pot (use cans if necessary for extra

weight, so the sandwich is compressed). Cook for 4 minutes on each side, until dark golden brown and crispy cheese, is melted.

6. Let sandwiches stand for 2 minutes before cutting them in half. Serve IMMEDIATELY.

# Cuban Chicken Noodle Soup

Cuba is known for its flavorful and unique cuisine, combining traditional Spanish and African influences. In particular, Cuban Chicken Noodle Soup is a favorite meal among both locals and visitors alike. This classic soup brings together tender pieces of chicken, a variety of local vegetables, and noodles in a rich broth that will warm you up on the coldest days.

Prep Time 17 mins Cook Time 1 hr 33 mins Total Time 1 hr 50 mins

## Ingredients

- ✓ 4 quarts of water
- ✓ 3 lbs bone-in chicken seasoned to taste with adobo or poultry seasoning
- ✓ 4 potatoes
- ✓ 1.5 cups carrots
- ✓ 3 cloves garlic
- ✓ 3 pieces ears of corn chopped into 4
- ✓ 3 tbsp sofrito
- ✓ 2 chicken bouillon
- ✓ 2/3 lb angel hair pasta
- ✓ salt and pepper to taste

## Instructions

1. Season the chicken with poultry seasoning or adobo.
2. Pour the water into a large pot, place the seasoned chicken in the water and cook for 50 minutes over medium-high heat.
3. Remove the chicken from the pot, remove the fat, and cut it into bite-sized pieces.
4. Place the chicken back in the pot along with the corn, carrots, garlic, and potatoes.
5. Stir in the chicken bouillon powder, sofrito, salt, and pepper.
6. Cover and cook for 50 minutes or until the vegetables are fork-tender.
7. Add the angel hair pasta and cook for 7 minutes.

8. Check for seasoning, serve with lime, and enjoy!

Made in United States
Orlando, FL
15 December 2024

55683422R00036